[i]

LOVE
MONEY
POWER

Proven 21st Century Money Methods
to Cultivate Successful Relationship

Cover design by SBG Media Group.

DEDICATION

This book is dedicated to women, men and couples of all shades and races, sizes, economic backgrounds and geographic locations. You are important because you exist. You are necessary to mankind for our world to grow.

FOREWORD

The world exists and evolves because we are living out our own live stories. Who would have thought, me, a real-life true storyteller? After releasing my book in 2017, Unveiling the Mask, I realized by giving my story back to the world freed me in a way I didn't know I was lost. I never considered myself a writer – but what I realized was as I was telling my story and writing my own book, that it was such an intimate relationship with the events of my past. It was almost more intimate than when certain events actually occurred. The freedom from sharing pieces of them was the best feeling and still is, almost ever. Professionally, I saw how much respect and credibility I gained by sharing authentically had given me as I continued to grow my business.

The purpose of this book is to improve the quality of millions of relationships all over the world. After looking at the numerous statistics, one can see that financial stress is a leading cause of divorce. In some cases, it ranked higher than infidelity. It is our desire to help other couples understand the complexities of what we call the "financial marriage" which can be more challenging that the physical marriage. We want to help couples work together to create a happy and successful financial relationship.

People place tremendous amounts of energy on money. When you combine two different individuals with different ideas or relationships with money, the effects can weaken or even destroy the best relationships. We discuss the relation with money and the relationship itself. Regardless of the type of relationship you are in, the concepts still apply.

I was inspired to write this book as a result of personal financial transformation and the financial struggles I've seen in other couples. In my own journey I come in contact with more and more women with their own stories. And not only did they have stories, but they wanted to be free too.

ACKNOWLEDGMENTS

God... Thank you for giving me all that you have – for trusting me with the charge of impacting the lives of your children in the way you would have me doing it. I am so grateful that you made my life so BIG and extend grace to me even in my humanness.

I must thank all of the co-authors of this anthology. They are the reason this book exists – their stories are necessary for our world to evolve.

Thank you to our Publisher for this project, Marilyn Porter. We truly could not have done this without you – you're amazing and I love you!

Thank you to my assistant, Briana White, for being my right hand. I know it's no small feat to work alongside me.

I have to thank my family and my extended family for being there for me in ways no one will ever know. It's because of them and my sacrifices that I am able to be who I am.

Thank you to Jerome Powell for being a great person for accepting that I will always be doing something bigger than the next – and the time it takes for me to make those things happen. You are a wonderful man – love you!

Last but not least, I have to thank my supporters, fans, clients and colleagues in my communities! I absolutely love you all and cannot live my truth without you.

DR. COZETTE M. WHITE

LOVE MONEY POWER

PROVEN 21ST CENTURY MONEY METHODS TO CULTIVATE SUCCESSFUL RELATIONSHIPS

MASTER YOURSELF TO WIN THE GAME OF LOVE!

SHEMIKA L. MERPHY
Financial Strategist

Society directly and indirectly shapes our points-of-views, perspectives and possibilities. People begin to succumb to societal norms and their expectations of life fall in line with what they've always seen and heard. So, with all the statistics, stereotypes, and status quo pointing to increasing divorce rates, both men and women have begun to accept their plight of never finding their partner in life because 'what's the sense' "experts say" and "numbers don't lie." The loudest conversation around divorces and breakups seem to always highlight infidelity but usually there is so much that is happening before or around the act of infidelity. Marriage counselors around the world find that the number one problem in relationships is not always infidelity but often stems from financial stress. Making this point is not to downplay infidelity and the effects it has on relationships; it is a real issue people face whether it is the primary issue or a reaction to other issues in a relationship. An extended conversation around increasing divorce rates are the conversations around unwedded successful women and men because as society would like to put it "more money, more problems" or that love is the sacrifice for success.

This all doesn't take away from the desire and need, of women and men alike, to love and be loved. Both men and women face the challenges of finding love with the right one. Online dating and matchmaker services to get to the one has become a $2.5 Billion booming industry but establishing a relationship that will stand the test of time and stress of finances should be an ongoing goal. So, it is imperative, with the amount of time and energy (and dare I say money) we put into finding someone, that we take the time to understand and instill what's necessary to cultivate and sustain a successful relationship. And since the number one strain to relationships and marriage has proven to be financial, the focus becomes how to win at Love AND Money.

Your personal relationship with money as well as money management skills can and will have a direct impact on your relationships; whether they be with your family, friends or significant others. If as an individual you work on your view and value of money, you are one step ahead in winning at the Love game. If you don't have a plan for your money as an individual it will be hard for you to stick to one with someone else. If you are in denial on where you stand with money, you will fall prey to the many pitfalls that money plays in tearing apart a marriage that was birthed from a loving relationship. It's important that you are willing to understand each other, your dreams, and your needs but most importantly be open and honest about sabotaging tendencies with money.

Getting to a place where you are able to be open and honest with yourself is often the path least taken; mostly because people don't do the self-work to increase their self-awareness or prefer not to as they equate it to being vulnerable. But getting to know yourself actually puts you in a place of power. Even better, in getting to know yourself you automatically learn how to better understand other people. So, if you can master who you are you can master money and master relationships. Before getting to the successful marriage, let's talk about some of the things you can do to be in position.

First thing first, what is your personality style and how does that tie into your money personality type, who you are in a relationship and who you need in a relationship.

Shemika Asks

What is your money personality; **analytical, amiable, expressive or driver?**

Knowing this about yourself and your significant other indicates if you are a thinker or a feeler and an introvert or extrovert;

- Amiable and expressive are feelers.
- Analytical and drivers are thinkers.

It's easier for feelers to be more in tune with nurturing relationships and they express their love well but are more free-spirited and may not be as grounded on handling money or making sound financial decisions. Thinkers are fact-focused and may not communicate or express their feelings well but will be more disciplined to achieve financial goals.

Next, getting to know more about your specific money personality and the type your significant other identifies with better equips to manage money together. Take the time not only to identify with the money personalities below but also understanding the behaviors that come with them in order to manage them when they show up in your relationship. Which money personality describes you and your significant other?

Amasser or Hoarder – *the size of the bank account matters and seeing a nice size nest egg gives a sense of security and achievement specifically for the amasser. So, if you are an amasser/hoarder or with one, know that spending money on stuff is probably not the primary ways you would show love or desire to receive love. So if you find that your significant other reacts to gifts* *with a simple thank you and quickly shifts to "how much did this cost?" or "You didn't need to spend all that money" don't take it personally or that they don't like the gift just know that he or she is just wired differently. The main difference between an Amasser and hoarder is their means of building a nest egg. Hoarders are less risk tolerant and will not be comfortable with risky investments they particularly just want to save while an Amasser likes the security of the nest egg but desires even more to see the savings grow and preferably at a fast rate. This makes them more risk tolerant and not as much of a worrier over money.*

Avoider – *talk about anything but money with the Avoider. Money Avoiders don't talk or think about money, so expecting them to be diligent in paying bills or having a budget would be setting yourself up for disappointment and lead to frustration. Understand that this is not just a* *matter of them being irresponsible but more of an insecurity. Trying to keep up with the ins and outs of money and balancing a checkbook is overwhelming to the Avoider and a daunting task they are just not good at. The best way to work with the Avoider is having the conversation at a high level and give them what they need to be successful at meeting the shared financial goal.*

Money Monk – *Money is the root of all evil for a monk. Their perspective is too much of it will corrupt you or lead to more problems. Amassing wealth is not even on their radar. But don't worry you won't be frustrated with their spending; it's their giving away that will cause financial friction. Giving isn't bad and the monk will likely not see anything wrong with helping others or using their money for important social and humanitarian causes even to the point of not having anything left for themselves. The best way to show your love to a Monk is by spending quality time with them and* *doing things with them that supports their need to help others. They appreciate the simpler things in life.*

Spender – *it's all about living your best life NOW! Spenders live their life in the moment and there is no cap on how much they will spend to have what they want right now. If this is your significant other or you are the spender in your relationship, understand that the nest egg is not what matters most, it's more about the material, status and experience of things. Gifts are welcomed, appreciated and preferred. Spontaneous expressions of love such as surprises will always be received with more enthusiasm than other acts of love. All is not lost with spenders you can for certain love and still achieve financial goals with your Spender because they tend to be driven at getting what they want, so your focus should be how to increase income in your household and putting a structure in place to ensure that before the "let the spending* *begin" kicks in all savings, investing and paying of bills are covered.*

Personality styles have always been focus points in the corporate world to develop leaders and cultivate productive working environments. It's a key part of developing employees to work well with each other and increase individual performance for corporate productivity goals. How this relates to Love, Money and Power? Well the methods used are the backbone to many personal development practices but taking those teachings to the next level by aligning them with your money personality type and being better in your personal relationships rarely happens.

Men and women around the world
strive to be their best at work,
in their communities, churches
and other associations
but many fail at being their best to
their significant others and allowing
them to be their best to you.

If you've ever sat wondering about the disconnect growing between you and your love, then the answer is in your Love Language and the one of your significant other.

Here are the 5 Love Languages by Gary Chapman:

1. **Words of Affirmation** - *some people need to here you say I Love You and how much they are appreciated. It's not the amount of gifts they receive but the amount of praise they receive. Acknowledgment of their efforts, their improvements, and accomplishments is what fuels love to and with the person that have words of affirmation as their go to.*

2. **Acts of Service** - *the old saying "actions speak louder than words' stands true for the*

men and women whose love language falls under acts of service. Just doing the small things for your love that helps them or acknowledges your understanding of their need of a helping hand and allowing them to feel like they are not carrying all the pieces by themselves speaks wonders. It lets them know that you care beyond doing things only for special occasions.

3. **Gifts** - gifts seems to be the go to for our significant others. Buying the pretty shiny things for the special occasions are the standard. But for the men and women who speak gift, they like to receive gifts just because. It's a way that shows you are being thought of or showing that you were thinking of him or her. It is even better received when it is a well thought out gift and shows you really pay attention to likes, dislikes and new interests. They can't wait to share with their

friends and family the newest expression of your love.

4. **Quality Time** – *time and attention is the name of the game. Beyond knowing that you are there, periodically spending uninterrupted time with you goes a long way. Quality time can look like an early morning walk together, sitting in a park to talk and listen to each other away from the typical noise of the day. Can someone say Stay-cation? It doesn't have to cost money because your time and attention is valued most to and with the person whose love language is quality time.*

5. **Physical Touch** – *affection is how you show love to the person whose love language is physical touch. "Touch me, squeeze me, kiss me and caress me" is what they are screaming at all times. So if your significant other speaks touch, opt to shower them with kisses*

than with elaborate gifts. An extra hug or a passionate kiss before you walk out the door will help them to take on their day with a smile or put an extra strut in their walk.

Knowing which love language speaks to you or your significant other most, empowers you to speak the right language to cultivate love in your relationship. Another plus is that you can save time and/or money by knowing. Although gifts is the go-to in relationships it's actually only one way to show love and it may or may not be the primary love language. In reality spending money on or for your significant other only works 50% of the time.

Here's another tip, if you're really good at one of these languages it might be time to learn a second language, so that you can exercise showing your love in your significant others secondary language.   Remember in most instances;

"Love don't cost a thing"

Once you have done the self-work and gained an understanding of how to respect the makings of other people you have empowered yourself to win in Love, Money, and Power.

"A life of Love,
Money and
Power isn't the
luck of a chosen
few!"

Shemika Advises

The greatest lesson I've learned is that the pursuit of happiness is a journey that should include a life of pursuing Love, Money AND Power simultaneously. Many may disagree and believe that you have to prioritize what you focus on at different points in your life. My point of view is that how much energy and time you put in those areas may differ but you should be continuously working on Love, learning how to love yourself, how to respect and love others, and how to receive love and respect from others. You should continuously be building a strong relationship with Money, pursuing it for a bigger purpose and giving your money an assignment for your life and the people in it. You should continuously be standing in your Power, exercising your God-given authority, empowering and equipping yourself to be all that you were created to be, and connecting with people of influence to use their power and resources to help you on this journey called life. At the center are Relationships. Relationships can be one of the greatest currencies you will ever earn and most valuable. Cultivating healthy relationships lead to Love (both self-love and attracting your Purpose Partner), Money (whether Job-offers and/or Business Opportunities) and Power (We've all heard the saying "it's not always what you know! There is even power in who you.

Finally, money is just the resource used to create the life you desire to live. You can choose to use it wisely, positively and purposefully. You have the power to create a life you love with each other and for each other.

BUDGETING FOR COUPLES

PATRINA DIXON
Certified Financial Educator

Money conversations are important for couples. In fact, they are one of the most important conversations that can be had – to avoid conflict in the area of finances. It should be discussed in various aspects. How much you have saved, (in liquid accounts, retirement or investments)? How do you manage money? What are your plans for money? How do you plan to grow it?

When planning a life together, couples must decide how money should best be managed in a combined household.

The two should be honest with each other and base their decision on the two of them and not on how their friends or family handles money. Couples complement each other in many ways and sometimes one is better at handling money than the other.

I have worked with people that have tried different ways to manage and budget money. And after setting certain methods in place, they must make modifications based on what they have learned along the way.

Step One

The couple should set up a household checking account where each can put money in, and the household bills can be paid.

Step Two

The couple should set up a combined savings account. It may be easier to have this savings account at the same bank as the household checking account, so when it is time to pay bills, a defined amount can be put into savings as well.

Step Three

Be sure each knows that income includes money from any paycheck from jobs each may have, revenue from a business, if either of them is an entrepreneur, child support, alimony, social security, state assistance, and any money either gets into the household.

Expenses includes mortgage or rent, electricity, gas, water, grocery, sanitation, taxes, house phone, cell phone, cable, and internet. It can also include car payment, car insurance, medical, dental, and vision insurance and going out to eat.

Here are a few methods to consider:

Even Split

Sit down together and look at all the income that comes into the household. Once that has been determined, review all the household expenses/bills. Take the total amount of expenses and cut it in half. Each person is responsible for their portion. This amount goes into the household checking account to pay all expenses/bills for the house. Each spouse must also put an equal amount in the savings account.

Percentage

Sit down together and look at all of the income that comes into the household. Once that has been determined review all the household expenses/bills. Take that total amount of expenses and split it via a percentage based on who makes more, e.g... if one makes more than the other, the one that makes more gets a higher percentage of the expenses (60%) and the other one gets the lesser percentage (40%). The money aligned to the percentages is put into a household account and paid accordingly.

<u>Divvy Responsibility</u>

The more dominant wage earner pays for the largest household bill, (usually the mortgage or rent), and the other pays for all the "other" household bills.

These methods can be used regardless of how frequently each gets paid. As some gets paid weekly, bi-weekly, twice a month and monthly. These methods are based on contributions for the monthly bills. Where this can be a bit tricky is when the deposit happens. Is it when either gets paid? Is it when bills are due? Is it at the end of the month or the beginning of the month?

Again, this must be determined on what is best for the household. What works best is when each deposits money into both the household bill checking account and combined savings account each time one gets paid, not to exceed the amount accountable per the method chosen.

Just like with your personal budget, the couple should use a resource both are comfortable with and know how to use. There are apps, free electronic editable budget sheets (www.itsmymoneyjournal.info/freebies), and hard copy 3-ring binder budget books. With so many tools available, the couple must agree on the tool. They must agree on who will complete the task of entering in the data in the chosen tool and choose who is going to complete the task to pay the bills or a combo of both.

The process of budgeting should be done every time one gets paid. This is also a good way to find where you can trim down on expenses so that you can work to lower expenses, make some change and use that extra money to save or invest.

Most find that tons of monies are spent on eating to eat and/or ordering out, gourmet coffee, or growing cable bill. This is when you can discuss how some of the things can be accessed for less as not to feel deprived of enjoying what you like, while rethinking how much you pay each month for them.

One important thing to note is there is no right or wrong way. When coming together as one, you try one way. If it doesn't work, try another. If that doesn't work, try another until you get to a place where both are comfortable of how the financial affairs are running for the household while saving money.

There are new resources for budgeting being created often, so continue to stay current with what is available and ensure there is transparency with the status of the household

budget and savings accounts.

Patrina Asks

1. Did you discuss finances with our partner early in your relationship?

_____

_____

_____

2. Do you and your partner share all finances and financial income and expenses with each other?

_____

_____

_____

_____

3. Do you only discuss larger financial purchases (maybe over a certain dollar amount) or income (a rate or bonus)?

_____

_____

_____

4. Do you all go over the bills together each month is one of you in charge of taking care of that   part?

_____

_____

_____

_____

"When you truly love

each other and tackle

the money journey

together it gives your

relationship power"

Patrina Advises

Here is a little bit more to give an answer to the question of What advice would you share about building a life filled with Love, Money and Power.

The best advice I can give is to be sure you have a good conversion about money, money habits, money goals and credit as you get into a serious relationship. You don't have to interrogate your potential husband or wife but ask thoughtful but productive questions about the topics. Their answers, better yet willingness to discuss the topics, will give you subtle indications. Please keep in mind that some people may be hesitant to discuss because they have not done well with their money however as long as they are open and honest and there is a positive and mutually understood at a path forward in the right lane that is a good sign. Remember, women - just because you may know more and have learned more along the way doesn't mean that a man that have not learned can't learn. For men, being the man of the house can include knowing who may be best to handle the money and bills. In some cases, it is both monthly or one or the other but be sure you both agree on the process so that someone is doing it. Review the income and expenses regular and discuss changes with either. It is also important to review and discuss opportunities for increase in income and reduction of expenses. Remember saving, budgeting, short- and long-term goals, life insurance and retirement must be a part of the plan. All of these things will make for a loving relationship, with money that make the two of you very powerful.

SINGLE
BUT
POWERFUL!

CARLENE RANDOLPH
Life and Relationship
Coach

Defining "singleness" is mind-blowing for some. Quite a few people would attempt to say there are several related behaviors that single folk display:

1) they are introverts

2) promiscuous

3) immature.

Some of us are none of these. Some are single at heart and living pretty fulfilled. We live in times that are so centered on married life even worse layering it with gender, ethnicity, socio-racial issues creating these impossible situations for people who do not fit the mold. To add to the equation, that happiness and success can only be attained through marriage or exclusive relationships.

Humans are social creatures. We thrive on connection, interaction, and unions with each other. As children, we are immediately and intimately connect to our parents or other nurturing adult. Further, we seek out our first playmates as early as two years old. Social acceptance in our peer group is key to our self-esteem throughout childhood. When the hormones begin to kick in as preteens and teenagers, the pursuit of romantic relationships becomes a central focus.

In our late teens and early twenties, in the modern Western culture, it is natural to begin thinking about finding a life partner. Some young adults have found "the one" (or at least the person they think is "the one") by the time they graduate from high school. Many more have done so by the time they graduate from college or reach their mid-twenties. Then again, many have not! In fact, more and more people are focusing less on long-term relationships in early adulthood and more on their friendships and career. "The average age of marriage in our culture continues to get older," as cited by Lenz in a 2013 study.

However, many are settling into commitment without marriage. There is still often a sense of urgency about finding a mate, a life partner, and perhaps starting a family, particularly among young women. There is the "biological clock" to consider for those who do want children, which can begin to tick noticeably sometime in the mid-twenties. Even for men, there may be social pressure, perhaps at a slightly older age, to "grow up," "be responsible," and find a life mate. That being said, there are differences between men and women at varying stages in their lives. The U.S. Census noted, "that there were roughly 52.3% of unmarried women over the age of 18 in 2016, while the percentage of unmarried men were in close range at 46.8%." Interestingly, singles in metropolitan areas have faced issues of lower numbers of possible mates due to lack of career opportunities, differences in education, and cultural complexities.

The "S" word...

In legal definitions for interpersonal status, a single person is someone who is not in a relationship or is unmarried. In common usage, the term 'single' is often used to refer to someone who is not involved in any type of serious romantic relationship, including long-term dating, engagement, marriage, or someone who is 'single by choice'. Single people may participate in dating and other activities to find a long-term partner or spouse.

People may remain single for a variety of reasons. These can be categorized in buckets: [1] personal (i.e. stress, health, or fear) or [2] professional (career, financial wellness, or education). Geographic location can also play a part in your singleness due to living in a society or locality where there is an insufficient number of people of the preferred sex for romantic or sexual attraction. Frankly speaking, one could simply suffer from extremely bad luck with finding anyone who will reciprocate an interest in a relationship. In some cases, single people have chosen their professional development and aspirations over marriage, domestic partnership, or other types of committed relationships.

The pressures of certain careers and positions require that people remain single. Sometimes, this is coupled with celibacy or chastity, either for secular or religious reasons, such as priests, nuns, and monks in certain faiths. Loneliness can occur for some people who look for but cannot find anyone they might wish to date, especially for those suffering the loss of companionship following divorce or bereavement. Some single people, however, regard and appreciate solitude as an opportunity.

As a single, young adult, the time will come for you when many of your friends are in committed relationships, living together, or getting married. What if you are still single? What if the relationship you had in high school or college did not end in commitment as you had originally hoped? What if you are 24, 38, or even 40 years old and you are not in a relationship or in an unsatisfying one that seems to be leading nowhere? Does the old adage "Always the bridesmaid, never the bride" seem like your motto? Are you one of the few true bachelors left at the bachelor parties? Do you feel like you need to be in a relationship to be considered normal or to feel good about yourself? Do you stay in a relationship just to avoid being single and alone? Alternatively, do you avoid relationships because you are fearful of commitment and find it hard to trust people?

Perhaps you are one of those people who are almost always in a relationship (one right after another) because you are afraid to do things without a partner. Do you feel that you may be left home alone on a Friday night if you do not have a partner? You may settle for unsatisfying relationships just to have a relationship and avoid feeling isolated.

On the other hand, you may be someone who is fearful of relationships and dating, so you avoid situations where people might be looking to attract someone. You stay at home or shy away from people who may be interested in you because you do not easily trust others and you fear intimacy. Maybe you are the type that is everyone's friend, but others do not see you as relationship material. You are always giving but not looking to get your own needs met. Therefore, others do not take you seriously as someone who is looking for a deeper connection. Maybe you are the type who is constantly expecting the next date (or next new person you meet) to be your soul mate. You try to go immediately into a deep connection, whether the other person is right for you or not. You move in too fast and too intensely, often scaring others away.

There are lots of benefits to being single and three of the benefits are discussed below:

Financial Freedom

While you may not have two incomes to pay your rent and bills and build your savings (or the tax break) as a single person, there are ways you can save money that a couple might not be able to. One of the financial benefits of being single is that your money and how you choose to spend it is completely, 100% in your control.

This kind of freedom can help guide your daily spending choices and those items (or trips) you splurge on.

While couples can split many costs, that doesn't put single women at a disadvantage. In fact, being single can be a huge advantage. When you're single, you never have to clear ideas with a second person and you never have to compromise. This makes decision-making a lot simpler and allows for extra savings opportunities.

Once you start to treasure your newfound freedom, you will realize that taking time for yourself will show you what is most important in your life. Enjoying your single time will make what you want clearer and reveal which areas of your life you should build upon. Additionally, studies show that experiencing something alone results in our brain forming a clearer and longer lasting memory.

Relationships take time and, to be frank, time is money. When you're coupled up, instead of coming home to a quiet apartment where you can sit down and concentrate on opportunities that bring in extra cash, you're often stuck figuring out what's for dinner, catching up on the day, and generally having less time to just "be". Take advantage of this free time by investing your energy into projects that could bring in extra income.

When you're single, your only debt is your own—unless you are a single parent. When you get married, regardless if you have separate accounts or not, you absorb all of your partner's debt, and you both become responsible for it on your taxes and your financial future in terms of buying a home, making big investments, and more. (Again, if you are a single parent, the aforementioned dynamic may still apply in relationship to you and your children.) A single person with independent finances has complete control over their financial destiny. They aren't restricted by any pre-existing financial requirements their partner may have, such as credit card debt or child support obligations.

Also, when you're single, you can make yourself financially strong before you get into a relationship. Though you may look forward to sharing your life with someone one day, it's important to make your own financial goals and plans. The most important financial rule a single person should follow is "become financially literate." Really understand your finances. Create and follow a budget, maximize your retirement benefits, pay down college debt, and spend as little as possible. This will help you spot and avoid getting into a relationship with a financial train wreck.

Dating is a great way to wave goodbye to all your hard earned cash. When you're with someone, there's nothing more important than impressing them, including by the use of your income. However, when the relationship fizzles, you realize how this tactic doesn't pay off. Not only are we more prone to spending when dating, married couples are more likely to have credit card debt than unmarried singles. So, don't get depressed when you're eating cheap meals alone. It's really a form of

investing in your future!

BEING SINGLE GIVES YOU OPPORTUNITY TO LOVE YOURSELF MORE

A lot of people get confused about the word "single." They don't know what it means, what it looks like, and how they're supposed to act during this "unfortunate state" they've found themselves in. To them, single is a status symbol meant to be escaped. It's a status you're not supposed to be comfortable in. It's a status that's just a step towards something better.

The people who think this way are what I like to call "Perpetual Daters." This breed of people don't understand that their relationship is a stage the same way single is. Both are relationships.

Perpetual Daters forget that being single is a choice, not a waiting period. They don't realize that just because there's not another person to devote their time to doesn't mean that their time isn't still devoted to someone.

For those of you who bounce from relationship to relationship with a few months alone in between partners, you have no idea what life is like once you've given up on the idea of a boyfriend or girlfriend as being the sole source of your happiness.

Contrary to popular belief, being single isn't about looking for love—or at least the kind you're used to looking for. Being single is as full of love as a relationship, even if it seems narcissistic to admit it because this relationship is about loving yourself just as much as you'd love someone else. It's about maturing as an individual, not a relationship and growing strong alone, rather than off someone. It's a completely new kind of a relationship that you will explore and discover the same way you would a new partner.

The best part about being single is looking for that one thing (or multiple things) that will absorb into and wrap itself around you. It's going to be something you miss and yearn for the way you did an ex-lover.

Only your passions will always love you back. They will never stray or leave you without warning. They will never become part of your life and then disappear. Your passions are the only things that should climb into bed with you before a man or woman. It's about giving love away without needing it back.

Being single isn't about looking for someone to love you, but rather looking for anything and everything to love. It's about loving everything you come in contact with. It's about forging relationships that don't need reciprocation and throwing you heart away without fear you won't get it back. It's about loving multiple people at one time while having a simultaneous love affair with your favorite books, movies and new passions. It's about making yourself a better person, not someone else.

Being selfish is only a problem when you're with someone. Being alone and worrying about yourself when you're single isn't selfish, it's necessary. Your life is completely and totally yours, with no one to take up your time or tell you you're wasting too much without them. Being alone and being in love with yourself is one of the most enviable relationships we can attain.

BEING SINGLE MAKES YOU STRONG AND POWERFUL

Letting go and moving on from a failing relationship will make us happier, healthier, and powerful. Of course, you don't want to see anyone hurt or disenchanted by the news to break off the relationship, but it may be the best decision for you both. Besides, life goes on and so, too, will your lives.

Here is a bit of advice:

- Do a periodic health check of your relationships.

- Decide if this is the relationship for you (be honest).

- Are you achieving your goals or dreams?

- Are you the person you always wanted to be?

When we let go, we fly. Even if we just take a couple of flaps and end up two feet away from where we were, not sure if we have the courage to try again, we still made a change — one that might have wide-ranging implications, if we just had the patience to let the ripples wash up against distant shores. My lesson in all this has been that taking the leap is always better, no matter how terrifying. In fact, the more terrifying it is, the more worthy the leap.

If you're contemplating making a big change, I say do it! The fear won't kill you (even if it feels like it might), but the consequences of not making that leap might be a lifetime of regrets. Really, what's the worst that can happen?

You have the power to change your destiny to live with gratitude and respect. Leave the door open for a successful next relationship and make a deposit into your love consciousness accounts by moving forward in love. There is "power" in letting go!

Now that you've had something to think about in regards to singleness and its benefits, let us briefly talk about why it's so important to move into healthier relationships with family, friends, co-workers, and romantic partners.

The honest truth is happy, healthy relationships have a healthy balance of stress. Sure, there is some give and take, but you always have security, honesty, and privacy between the parties in the relationship. For example, he decided to ensure that the coffee maker was prepped and ready for his partner daily, but what mattered most is that he encouraged his significant other to talk about what has challenged their day to day lives with one another. It was a chance to make a good impression and reinforce the trust and respect they had for one another.

Know yourself and what it takes to please you. Be honest about that information with your prospective partner, whether in your personal or professional life. Work through the difficult times with the idea that each person is able to be themselves without retribution. Relax and enjoy the silence together or be playful when the situation calls for changing challenging issues to allow comfort for all. Recognize that defining what it means to be in a committed relationship and making the most of your difference will greatly improve your experiences together and apart.

In conclusion, there is nothing inherently wrong with being single, and there is nothing inherently good about being in a relationship. Whatever your situation, it is crucial to look at what being single means to you and what a healthy relationship would look like. It is possible to have a fulfilling and happy life as a single person, and it is obvious that many couples are not happy, as evidenced by the high divorce rate and number of domestic disputes. However, given our social nature, it is common to desire a relationship and to share your life with someone. Finding the right person for this type of union cannot be scheduled or planned.

The key to establishing a healthy and happy relationship is to love oneself as a single and autonomous human being first; then seek out a relationship, only to add to richness to one's life — not to complete oneself as a person. Allow time to fully know yourself so that you do not become absorbed in a relationship, like a chameleon who simply adjusts to whatever or whoever is around him or her. Become comfortable with yourself and your aloneness. Ultimately, each of us is alone. No other person can fully know and understand us or take away our existential loneliness. Sure, being in a relationship can keep loneliness at bay, but eventually, we all come to the realization that no one else can feel our pain, think our thoughts, or carry all of our burdens. To get comfortable with oneself means to be at peace with being alone. It means not always needing someone to understand us, nor always needing another's company to make us feel safe or at peace. It means not counting on one person, or even several, to take away difficult or negative feelings, such as sadness, anger, or grief. To enter into a relationship in a state of independence will allow the relationship to add meaning and depth to your life. On the contrary, if you enter a relationship needing someone to hold you up, take away your loneliness, assuage the hard feelings, or make you feel complete, the relationship is sure to eventually bend and break under the pressure. Then, you will not only have an ailing self-esteem and loneliness to deal with, you will have added heartache of a breakup to your troubles and likely intensified the first two!

REFERENCES

"Single By Choice – Boston Magazine". 3
January
2012.

AFP/Discovery News, January 12, 2010Alex
Williams, "The New Math on Campus",
New York Times, February 5, 2010

Kislev, Elyakim. (2017-09-01). "Happiness,
Post-
materialist Values, and the Unmarried".
Journal of Happiness Studies. 0 (0): 1–
23. Doi:10.1007/s10902-017-9921-7. ISSN
1573-7780.

"Single living is the new way to find
happiness".
Times Online. August 3, 2005. Retrieved
June 2, 2010.

Schefft, J (2007). Better Single Than Sorry.
Harper

    Collins.

A b "Health Benefits Of Being Single".
Huffpost

    Healthy Living. February 12, 2013.

Lenz, L. (2016, August 31). When do people in
    your state get married? The Daily Dot.
    Retrieved from
    https://www.dailydot.com/irl/average
    -age-marriage-by-state/

U.S. Census Bureau. (2017, August 14). *FFF:*
    Unmarried and Single Americans Week:
    Sept. 17-23, 2017 (Release Number:
    CB17-TPS.62) .Washington, DC: U.S.
    Government Printing Office

UNCOVER MONEY PERSONALITIES AND HOW THEY IMPACT RELATIONSHIPS

PIA WASHINGTON
Relationship Coach

I am married to my junior high school sweetheart Levett and at the time of this writing we just celebrated our 25th wedding anniversary. As with many couples, we are complete opposites. He is a social, outgoing and always the life of the party. He is also an adventurous risk taker. I am a natural introvert, cautious, conservative and very risk averse. In many ways we complement each other and there is a sense of balance and teamwork that comes from our unique skills, behaviors and personalities. However, there are often times when our differences can cause conflict, misunderstanding and resentment. A good example of this is our love languages. Dr. Chapman, author of The Five Love Languages, suggests that people tend to naturally give love in the way they prefer to receive love and as a result we all have primary and secondary love languages. My husband's love languages are gifts and acts of service and my love languages are physical touch and quality time. Simply identifying your love languages is not enough. As a couple you must understand and learn to communicate and demonstrate caring to the other person in the love language the recipient understands.

In the same way that we all have different love languages, each of us views money and finances in a unique and highly personal way and as a result we have a different money personality or spending style.

Similar to love languages, you may have a primary or secondary style and there is no right or wrong. Each style has its own strengths and weaknesses. Your money personality is how you view money and the lens through which you make financial decisions. The goal in discovering your spending style is to help you understand yourself and the way you think about money because the more you know about yourself and your perspective on money the better equipped you are to work with your spouse to build a strong money relationship.

Money and stress go hand in hand for many Americans, whether they are in relationships or not.

A study by the American Psychological Association found almost three-quarters of Americans are experiencing financial stress at least some of the time, and nearly a quarter of us are feeling extreme financial stress. Different views and values regarding money can be a particular source of tension within couples. Approximately 63% of couples think their significant other overspends in some way and a study published by the National Council on Family Relations found money

fights are the top predictor of divorce. Financial infidelity, which is defined as lying, hoarding, hiding money or controlling money, is on the rise in couples. What can seem like a little "white lie" or small omission by one person can be seen by their partner as a huge breach of trust.

Although research shows "money" is the #1 cause of divorce in America, it is not necessarily lack of money that causes problems. Often times it is financial infidelity or the inability to communicate effectively about our money beliefs and values. Problems also arise when one of you neglects to hear the other persons input or refuses to participate in any financial decision-making. Let's face it; people spend more time planning their wedding than they do their marriage. Couples need to have real conversations and address the issues that influence how they save, spend, invest, give away money or go into debt. The good news is that if you are reading this book you must be open to developing new patterns of communication. You can learn to work together, make decisions without arguing and develop positive strategies for your money relationship and your financial future as a couple.

The first step is to identify your money personality. There are several resources available for you, but I have developed a quick test to help you identify your primary spending style. Once you've determined yours, it is important to learn that of your partner, parents, kids or anyone with whom you have a financial relationship. And just like the love languages, it doesn't stop with identifying the differences. The next and most important step is to seek to understand the other person's style and learn how you can work together and make financial decisions in a peaceful and productive way.

Most of us have a general idea of whether we are a spender or a saver, but it's imperative to dive deeper and determine what drives that behavior, how it manifests in your life and its impact on your relationships.

Pia Asks

Here are a few questions for you to ask yourself to begin to uncover your money personality;

1. What are a few of your first money memories?

   _____

   _____

   _____

2. Were they happy or sad memories?

   _____

   _____

   _____

3. What was your experience with money as a child?

_____

_____

_____

4. Did you have an allowance?

_____

_____

_____

5. Did you have a job or get paid for chores?

_____

_____

_____

6. If you had money, were you allowed to spend it freely?

_____

_____

_____

7. What messages did you get as a child about earning, spending, saving and giving money?

_____

_____

_____

8. What was your first big purchase? How did you pay for it?

_____

_____

_____

9. Who made the big financial decisions in your family?

_____

_____

_____

10. Who paid the bills?

_____

_____

_____

11. Who gave you money?

_____

_____

_____

12. Were there fights about money in your

home? If so, how did that affect you?

_____

_____

_____

13. What is your worst fear concerning

money?

_____

_____

_____

14. Do you expect that a life partner should

support you or that you should be self-

sufficient?

_____

_____

_____

15.How much would you spend without
telling your partner?

_____

_____

_____

Now that you have given some thought in how
your money personality may have developed
over time, let's take a deeper dive and identify
your spending style. Please keep in mind that
we all may have a little of each style but there
should be one that stands out among the rest
as the most dominate or primary style. Ask
yourself the following questions and

determine which one describes you the best.

Another way to think if it is, how would your

closest friends and family answer the question

about you.

What is your Spending Style?

Is money is used to create a positive image of yourself?

1. **The Status Seeker – money is used to create a positive image.**

Strengths
- Generous,
- Impressive;
- Weaknesses:
- Superficial,
- Insensitive

Impact to Relationships

The status seeker presents a strong first

impression. You tend to give expensive or

unexpected gifts and are appreciated for your generosity. You may also be perceived as "well to do" or wealthy because you buy name brand items with a high price tag. Others would describe you as competitive, pretentious or superficial.

One of the main concerns with the Status Seeker is that you may feel a constant need to keep up with the Joneses which can be stressful if you cannot afford it. The status seeker usually does not set aside money for savings or for emergencies and may go into debt to support their spending habits. Because they often spend money to feel good or validated, they often associate their extravagant possessions with self-worth. You may keep money secrets because of the fear of losing friends or status if others know your real financial situation.

Strategies for Success

If "Status" is your dominant money personality, you need to set up automatic savings and online payments so that you can pay yourself first and make sure all of the bills get paid on time. Don't spend money unwisely to maintain appearances. Shopping is ok if you set a budget, make lists and shop for quality, not name brands. If you have too much debt (credit card usage over 30%); talk to a financial professional to learn how to pay

it off as quickly as possible. Lastly, support

yourself with positive affirmations that you

are a lovable, valuable person.

2. Is money used to enjoy the moment and
carefree lifestyle?

Strengths
- Fun-loving
- Daring easygoing
- Weaknesses
- Impulsive
- Irresponsible

Impact to Relationships

The spontaneous spender enjoys adventures

and the unexpected. You are typically very

social and have many friends and acquaintances that will join you in your fun-seeking activities. Your fun-loving personality means you are the life of the party and you often pick up the check for your whole group. You like the thrill of taking risks and are usually not concerned with money details or the consequences of overspending. Others describe you as impulsive, social and carefree. Often the spontaneous person will spend money even when they don't have it or go into debt to buy things you need because they failed to plan. This can be concerning to a partner especially when the spending is out of control or if the person begins to keep money secrets from significant others. In some cases they are so carefree that they may even lose track of money or possessions.

Strategies for Success

The most important strategy for the Spontaneous is to continue to find things to do socially that

are free or very inexpensive. Plan any of the activities ahead of time and budget for them. Try splitting checks instead of picking up everyone else's tab. Learn simple techniques to make a basic budget and keep track of your money. If you live with someone who pays the bills, go over a month's expenses to be familiar with basic costs. If you have investments of inherited money, make an appointment with a financial professional to find out how much money you have and how it is being managed.

3. Does money help you feel good by giving to others?

Strengths

- Thoughtful
- Charitable
- Service-oriented
- Weaknesses
- Enabling
- Martyr

Impact to Relationships

Supportive givers donate generously to people or charitable causes. You typically have strong values and can be counted on to act with integrity. Family and friends appreciate your thoughtfulness, compassion and generosity. Others describe you as dependable, generous and caring.

Unfortunately, givers may be taken advantage of financially or become an enabler. Loved ones may perceive your gifts as a way to control them or impose your personal values on them.

Overextending yourself or sacrificing the needs your family for others can cause issues between you and your partner.

Strategies for Success

The key to success and creating balance for the giver is to develop a plan of how much you will give vs. invest in you your future and stick with the plan. It is important to understand that having

money is not inherently bad or sinful and being poor is not necessarily honorable. Before helping others consider if you may be enabling them or limiting their growth. Make sure you identify your own needs, wants and desires before you sign up to help someone else with their goals.

4. Does money help you feel safe and achieve goals?

Strengths
- Responsible
- Conservative
- Thrifty
- Weaknesses
- Suspicious
- Cheap
- hoarder

Impact to relationships

If you identify with the secure saver you are a planner with a budget, financial goals, and substantial savings. You protect money by being conservative and often times will only buy things on sale. You are disciplined,

[112]

practice delay gratification and understand the importance of setting aside money for an emergency fund. Others describe you as cautious, responsible and analytical.

Your strict budget may prevent you from participating in certain activities or taking advantage of certain unexpected opportunities. You are risk averse and may be sacrificing growth for security in your investments. Often times you will resent others who do not share your value for security and may have difficulty in relationships with spenders. Secure savers feel the need to take control of the finances and/or plan all of the expenditures.

Strategies for Success

Consider revising your budget to set aside more money for entertainment, gifts and other social activities. Take a break from being productive and goal – oriented to relax, enjoy life and experience new activities that are outside of your comfort zone. Challenge yourself to make sure your goals reflect your wants and needs and not just the basic needs. Work with a trusted financial professional to make sure you are incorporating the appropriate amount of risk in your investment portfolio.

Identifying your spending style gives you insight into why you think the way you do about money but more importantly, knowing your partner's spending style gives you insight into them. The more you learn how to communicate in each other's language, the more successful your

relationship will be in the long run. In our marriage, I am a secure saver and my husband is a spontaneous spender. Subconsciously, I may be drawn to the risk taking of the spontaneous spender because he brings the thrill of the unknown into my otherwise predictable life. Similarly, a status seeker may be attracted to the supportive givers generosity and so on.

Now that you understand your individual spending styles, how they impact relationships and some strategies for success it is time to put that knowledge into action. Because money personalities are rooted in values they are unlikely to change. Values refer to stable life goals that people have and reflect what is most important to them. They are established throughout one's life as a result of the accumulating life experiences and tend to be relatively stable. The values that are important to people tend to affect the types of decisions that they make, how they perceive their environment and their actual behaviors. Early family experiences are important influences over the dominant values. A good example of a value would be security.

So keep in mind that the goal here is to seek first to understand, not to change your partners spending style. Practice effective communication techniques that you can use when your significant other's money personality conflicts with your values and goals. It is equally important to be tolerant and patient of their values, Try to see things from their perspective and understand where they are coming from. Remember that marriage is a partnership, not a dictatorship and it is all about finding common ground and balance.

Some of our most intense arguments have been about how we deal with money. I had to learn early on in our marriage to be okay with him offering to pick up the tab when we are out with friends. The way that I deal with this is to make sure we have a large enough entertainment budget and contingency so that when we go out we can both enjoy ourselves and have a stress-free evening. He has had to learn to make sure he informs me of large expenditures, in our case, anything over $500 so that I can make sure it is accounted for. We also both agree to pay ourselves first and have a significant amount of our savings and investments for our retirement automatically deducted from our checks and our bank accounts. In the end, you have to keep in mind that marriage brings together two individuals from different backgrounds with two completely unique ways of thinking. No matter how much you love one another, merging your lives — and your money — can be a beautiful (but bumpy) ride. With love, understanding and effective communication you can have a strong and healthy relationship

and live your very own happily ever after.

Cai and Shemika Wrap It Up!

Most couples would wish to save money and secure their future. However, many of the couples are unwilling to hear financial advice from any experts. The major reason is that they know that since their earnings are finite, savings would most likely entail a form of cutbacks that they would be uncomfortable with. Moreover, the emergence of social media has made many couples want to live like the 'other couple' they see. The truth is, many successful couples, or even people in general, had or are still taking savings as a serious component of their lives. This chapter is designed to instill the necessary skills and attitudes for a couple to acquire a culture of savings.

Any person earning an income has the potential to save.

The process requires a person to ensure that his/her spending should not exceed his/her earnings.

The decision to save might not only lead to a stronger relationship but could also facilitate a couple in achieving their dreams.

Here are a few tips to cultivate a successful marriage with your spouse and partnership in achieving money goals.

1. Create a shared vision

The key to winning at the money game in marriage and any relationship is creating and being committed to a shared vision and goals. Couples often make the mistake of going overboard to proving they haven't lost themselves in marriage and are still individuals. But in order for relationships to work, it requires you not only to say you are together but act like your together and dream together. Achieving a shared vision requires setting up a time to plan for strategic thoughts as you move together.

Some questions that can assist couples in planning are;

- What do we want in the short-term (1 year)?

- Middle-term (1-5 years)?

- Long-term (over 5 years)?

- Who are we as a couple? This question is particularly important if a couple has never had a shared vision before.

- How can we improve our marriage/union?

- What experiences do we want in a period of time?

It might appear frivolous but make sure that you write your plan as a couple. Research has shown that there is an 80% more chance for an individual to follow through on something that is written (Les and Parrot, 2018).

When your dreams and desires for your lives are in sync it's less of a tug of war with getting your significant other on board.

2.   Set goals and the plan of action together

You've probably heard the saying "a goal not written down is just a wish." A shared vision requires action to become a reality. Set small goals towards milestone achievements. As a couple, you should commit to the action steps or changes each of you are willing to take to achieve them. The goals set would enable the couple to achieve their visions. While setting goals, couples, should work at ensuring they set SMART goals. That is, the goals set should be Specific, Measurable, Attainable, Realistic and Time-based (Amberly, n.d). Specific is equivalent to a mission statement of a company. When thinking of specific goals think of the popular W questions including Who, What, When, Where, Which, and Why. Measurable means that the goal has specific metrics that could be used to gauge if the goal is successful. Achievable implies that the goal could be achieved using the available resources. A common mistake couples make is designing goals with the anticipation that resources would emerge from somewhere in the future. Relevant means that the goal should be consistent with the couple's overall vision. Finally, goals need to be time-bound such that couples have a deadline.

After setting the goals, it is imperative for couples to set a plan of action of achieving the goals. Often, a plan of action would require sacrifice and commitments from the couple. For instance, if the couple intends to purchase a house in five years, they may need to sacrifice some expenditure such as an overseas vacation. A couple should take time in discussing and agreeing on the role of each partner in executing the actions.

3. Lay the foundation and structure to support your shared vision

An important part of two becoming one is not the reciting of the vows but actually operating as one unit. Most couples think that as long as they assign who pays the different household bills they are doing a good job at managing their finances. But keeping all things separate including how you pay bills and contribute to your shared vision is one of the mistakes most couples make. How do you avoid this mistake? Combine your finances in a joint account. It's not about who pays what or how much you save individually but achieving your goal as a unit. This also creates a level of transparency and accountability with one another. That is not to say that couples should not have separate accounts. In ideal settings, couples should have joint accounts for shared goals and some separate accounts to allow for some independent spending.

4. **Have periodic checkins on your goals** Couples typically don't talk about their finances until there's a problem. A bill wasn't

paid, your overdrawn or overextended, or you can't afford to do or have something you really want. This mistake is probably at the core of the issue of money in marriages. Taking the time to sit together and go over finances allows you to catch things before they get too far off the track of the shared vision and also the opportunity to acknowledge and celebrate your milestone wins so the conversation around money is not always a bad one or highlighting the negatives. This again creates transparency and accountability to stay committed.

The idea of monitoring goals is to evaluate if the plan of action is on the right track. Couples should be flexible when they notice some things are not working out. Couples should remember that life is unpredictable and certain things, such as changes in income levels, could affect an initial plan. Also, it is possible for a couple to change their vision. Couples should not fear to redesign their plans to fit their current circumstances (For Your Marriage).

5.   Remember comparison is the thief of joy

In a marriage one may make more money than the other, whether it's by a small or significant amount, it's important to not devalue the other's contribution to the household or shared vision. This also applies to your individual financial standing. One may come into the relationship or marriage with better credit, less debt or more savings, it's important to not see that as giving that person more power or say in the relationship. Consider this as a positive positioning for you as a couple and one less obstacle you have to face as a team. This can be an important tip for the successful men and women out there that may make more money than their spouses. Refrain from talking about finances in the manner of "what I bring in versus what you bring in" but value the

contribution to the shared vision equally.

Oracles (2017) 10 Sacrifices Successful People

    Make for Their Dreams. *Oracles*.
    https://www.success.com/10-sacrifices-successful-people-make-for-their-dreams/

The Work

1. Identify the need for discussing finances in a relationship

Learners will appreciate the importance of discussing finances. Early in a relationship, a couple should identify their financial direction to determine how bills and debts are going to be paid. It has been established that most couples avoid discussing finances in details. However, earnings are limited for most people and developing a financial plan is better than not developing it. After all, failing to plan is planning to fail. Couples who avoid financial planning would often fight about finances later in the relationship.

2. Recognize savings as a pertinent financial issue

Savings improves security in a relationship. A couple with savings is able to bounce back after an unexpected event occurs in their life, and these events often occur. Savings also makes couples achieve their dreams. It is vital for couples to agree on their dreams and ambitions before starting a saving project. One partner's dream is not necessarily the dream of another partner. Ideally, each couple should save at least for emergencies.

3. Understand the need for Joint and Separate accounts for couples

Some experts advise that couples should have only joint savings accounts so that 'surprises' are minimized in the marriage. While that is a piece of sound advice, this course advocates that couples should have both joint and separate accounts. The joint accounts should be for the projects that the couples agree that they will undertake together. They would be the main targets for the couples' savings. However, having separate accounts give the partners the freedom to spend their money on what they individually want. Although a couple should ideally work as a unit, we believe that some obligations and expenses are best handled at an individual level. The choice of the account types will depend on the couple's aspirations in the long run.

4. Appreciate the role of savings in building wealth

Learners will appreciate how savings could enable an individual with normal earnings could build wealth over time. It is important for learners to understand that savings and sacrifice go hand in hand. Learners will also appreciate the cases of how successful people sacrificed their expenses to achieve their goals. Each or one of the partners should be ready to forego an expense or expenses if they are to start saving.

5. Develop a habit of saving money

The course believes that saving is a habit that can be acquired even by those with limited knowledge on it. The idea of living from one paycheck to the next should be discouraged as it often leads to instant instability in the case of emergency-like expenses or events. Some methods fronted that could enhance the development of the habit of saving money in couples include:

- Automating the finances such that the savings are done automatically from the bank

- Developing a spending barrier that prevents impulse buying

- Agreeing on priorities while spending money

- Developing specific money goals

- Believing that they deserve to acquire wealth

- Ensuring that all the spending is tracked

- Paying their high-interest rate debts first

Outcomes and assessment criteria

The assessment method will include the learners' participation during the sessions. The criteria for assessments are included below:

Outcomes	Assessment criteria
	To achieve each outcome, the learner must demonstrate the ability to:
1. Identify the need for discussing finances in a relationship	Describe the role of financial discussions in relationship
	Identify the importance of planning about spending
	Explain how financial issues might bring about fights and disagreements
2. Recognize savings as a pertinent financial issue	Explain the role of savings in attaining financial freedom
	Describe why the couples' goal needs to be in sync before embarking on savings
	Describe how the decision to save can also bring issues in a relationship
3. Understand the need for Joint and Separate accounts for couples	Explain the benefits and shortcomings of joint accounts in relationship
	Explain the benefits and drawbacks of separate accounts
	Describe the rationale for using both the separate and joint accounts in achieving savings
4. Appreciate the role of savings in building wealth	Discuss the concept of sacrifice in the quest of attaining savings
	Appreciate how successful people are able to acquire savings
5. Develop a habit of saving money	Explain why savings can be described as a habit
	Appreciate the role of automation in promoting a savings culture
	Describe how impulse buying is an impediment to saving
	Identify the roles of prioritizing on spending patterns
	Appreciate the role of tracking finances in financial management
	Explain the rationale of paying high-interest loans first

Discussion activities

Why do couples fear to discuss their finances?

_____

_____

_____

What is the role of financial planning in a

stable and healthy relationship?

_____

_____

_____

Is savings important in any relationship?

_____

_____

_____

What are the drawbacks that could be faced
by couples who only use joint accounts?

_____

_____

_____

How can a couple address the drawbacks
faced by joint accounts?

_____

_____

_____

What types of expenses are best handled by

separate accounts?

_____

_____

_____

What sort of emergencies can make a couple

without savings wish they had one?

_____

_____

_____

What is the role of automation in encouraging

savings?

_____

_____

_____

How can tracking expenses help in savings?

_____

_____

_____

What are the risks faced by a couple who

avoid savings?

_____

_____

_____

References

Amberly (n.d). Making marriage a priority
throughout every stage of life
https://www.aprioritizedmarriage.com
/blog/goal-setting-in-marriage

For Your Marriage. Set Goals for Your
Marriage.
http://www.foryourmarriage.org/blog
s/set-goals-for-your-marriage/

Les, D. and Parrot, L. (2018). Building a
shared
vision in your marriage: 3 questions to
answer. Symbis
https://www.symbis.com/blog/buildi
ng-a-shared-vision-in-your-marriage-3-
questions-to-answer/

The Visionary

COZETTE

DR. COZETTE M. WHITE is an acclaimed bestselling author, nationally recognized accounting and tax strategist, international speaker and philanthropist. She inspires individuals to live in purpose, embrace passion, and achieve personal greatness through a balance in work and life.

White has been coined "Your Financial Physician" as a result of her unparalleled ability to empower her clients to ditch debt and develop a plan to create the kind of wealth that leaves a secure financial legacy.

[148]

She's able to diagnose negative money stories and provide a cure to transform limited beliefs to the sky's the limit! White prescribes the right Financial Rx to boost your financial health.

Dr. White has more than 20 years of experience in corporate America. In her roles, she was responsible for the financial affairs of the organization and focused on a broad range of financial, operational, strategic and executive leadership issues impacting the organization. During her tenure, Dr. White was instrumental in developing processes to ensure that Sarbanes-Oxley (SOX) protocols were in compliance with company standards and were maintained within the business.

Dr. Cozette M. White is the Founder and CEO of My Financial Home Enterprises a global firm providing comprehensive accounting, tax and business management services for businesses and individuals. Our specialized services allow us to focus on your financial needs to keep your business profitable, while you stay focused on your clients or patients. My Financial Home has been featured in Forbes Magazine and named one of The Boss Network's top 50 companies two years in a row. As Cameka Smith, Founder and CEO of the Boss

Network put it, *"without question she is brilliant at teaching others to leverage their unique gifts and qualities into a financial windfall."*

White received her Master of Business Administration degree from the University of La Verne and her Bachelor of Science degree in Accounting from California State University, Dominguez Hills. Later Dr. White was awarded a Doctorate Degree of Philosophy Letters. She is involved in her community and is a member of

[150]

Alpha Kappa Alpha Sorority, Inc., and she is a member of the National Association of Black Accountants. Additionally, Dr. White is the Founder and Executive Director of Achieving My Dreams Foundation, Inc., a non-profit organization that provides scholarships to graduating high school seniors.

Dr. White is a resident Money Matters Expert for FOX40's Studio40 LIVE and her advice has been called upon by CBS This Morning, NBC, ABC and FOX television stations. She has been featured on the numerous radio shows including Radio One and iHeart radio, she's a recurring voice to millions making regular appearances in various national media outlets, including Black Enterprise, Forbes, Women of Wealth, Upscale, The Huffington Post, and countless newspapers across the country.

Dr. Cozette's personal and professional achievements have not gone unnoticed, and through the years she has been awarded:

- 2019 Top 28 Business Influential Pioneer by K.I.S.H. Magazine

- 2019 Dynasty of Dreamers by K.I.S.H. Magazine

- 2018 Top Business Award by The Boss Network

- 2018 Top Female Expert by Huff Post

- 2018 Bestseller Author - 'Unveiling the Best'

- 2017 Top Business Award by The Boss Network

- 2017 Lifetime Achievement Award by President Barack Obama

- 2017 Bestseller Author - 'Attracting the Best'

- 2017 10 Women Speakers to Know - Jazzy Creative Magazine

- 2017 Top 6 Leaders of The Month - WomELLE Magazine

- 2016 Wealth Builder Extraordinaire by Women of Wealth Magazine

Get your transformation started today by contacting Dr. White.

CONTACT COZETTE

Email cozette@cozettemwhite.com

SHEMIKA

SHEMIKA L. MERPHY an authority in Financial Planning Strategy, is a well sought after Mentor, Coach, Consultant and Speaker that is gifted in empowering those she comes across to achieve their personal and financial goals. She is the Founder and CEO of SOLIDifynancial, Inc., a financial management and advisory firm where the mission is to increase the net worth and build generational wealth for clients. She has always been known for her solid financial position and her sound financial advice; She is The Net Worth StrategistTM, Your Wealth SOLIDifierTM that not only talks the talk but walks the walk by using strategies of the wealthy to change the financial lives of the Middle Class and aspiring Entrepreneurs.

Shemika's commitment to her clients is to strengthen their financial literacy, money management skills, inspiring them to pursue wealth and enlightening them on the resources available to make money, grow money and keep money. She has provided tax preparation, financial planning services and wealth strategies for the past 11 years which has resulted in her proven ability to eliminate debt of over $200K, increase credit scores by 100 – 250 points, increase savings by 10% – 20% and increase the net worth of her clients to $375K.

Shemika is an avid learner that's committed to forever being a student seeking to continuously grow as a person and in her passion. It is true to say that she has always been a person that offers solutions rather than focusing on the problem. Shemika has more than 10 years experience working in Corporate America in the New York Metro area. Her professional career consists of working in Insurance Fraud at a Wall Street Law Firm, Financial Accounting and Project Management for S&P 500 companies where she has managed multi-million dollar projects and implemented business process improvements for cost-savings, and an Independent Consultant in Financial Services. She is a graduate of Long Island University, where she received her Masters of Science in Accounting. She has also received Accounting certifications from the public accounting firm, PriceWaterHouse & Coopers and Auditing certifications from the International Auditors Association (IAA).

Recently she has been appointed as the Treasurer of an international women's association, became a contributing Author to the Love Money Power book anthology and a registered Investment Advisor Representative.

Shemika currently resides in the New York Metro area and outside of embracing her life's purpose, she enjoys traveling for exotic vacations, watching movies, dancing and relaxing on her own or with close friends and family.

CONTACT SHEMIKA
Email: Shemika@shemikamerphy.com

PATRINA

PATRINA DIXON is a Certified Financial Education Instructor, International Speaker and an Award-Winning Author of the top-selling financial guided series, "It'$ My Money™". Patrina is a 2018 100 Women of Color Honoree. Patrina is an advocate for financial literacy. She has a passion for serving her community and uses her company, P. Dixon Consulting, LLC to offer money management strategies to people ages 24-60. Patrina is shaping the spending and saving behaviors of her clients with a goal of guiding them toward financial independence. Patrina shares financial content as a blogger and through her podcast, The Money Exchange. Through her education received at the University of Hartford's Barney School of Business and the disciplines she learned while achieving her Financial Management Certificate from Cornell University allows her to thrive at teaching the importance of financial independence. The It'$ My Money™ journal book series and workshops allows Patrina to educate and enlighten youth and families on their finances. She is dedicated to molding the next set of financial leaders. Patrina is a devoted wife and mother who resides in Connecticut.

CONTACT PATRINA

Email: patrina@itsmymoneyjournal.info

CARLENE "CAI" RANDOLPH is a Personal Growth Strategist. Cai broke away from the mold of federal employee to forge a pathway to health, relationship, life and strategic leadership coaching because of feeling that serving others was the key to her success. Eventually, Coach Cai, discovered a way to share her passion as a mentor, coach, radio host and speaker. She held many leadership roles in the federal government for over 20 years and recently founded Caism, LLC, to expand her own programs. Cai never thought she would stand before women leading them through empowerment sessions with such confidence. She has been referred to as "Mama C" by her audiences because of her inspiration and nurturing strength. Over the years, Coach Cai, experienced

[160]

broken relationships, the loss of loved ones, serious illness among many life situations and found that the depth and breadth of these lessons learned were similar to those whom she coached. She created a system to help others through the singleness process. Prior to co-authoring the book "Love, Money and Power," Coach Cai, empowered women in groups and workshops. Her vision is to offer women simple solutions in chaotic times to assist them in releasing their best lives, through forming a community, building networks and providing them related resources.

CONTACT CARLENE

Email: caismisalifestyle@gmail.com

PIA

PIA WASHINGTON is a best-selling author, speaker and financial consultant from Los Angeles, California. Author of _Attracting the Life You Want from the Boardroom to the Bedroom_, she is dedicated to helping people produce extraordinary results in their relationships, finances and careers.

She is a results-oriented professional with over 25 years of experience across a wide range of industries such as Real Estate, Media & Entertainment, Technology, Biotech, Retail, Financial Services and Manufacturing. As a finance executive, she has achieved results for many Fortune 500 companies including NBC Universal, DineEquity, Amgen, Guitar Center, Exxon Mobil and Eaton Corporation. In 2018, she was awarded the _Above and Beyond_ Award from NBC Universal for her dedication to their Business Planning & Consolidations Program.

Her most important and rewarding role is that of loving wife and mother. She has been happily married to her junior high school sweetheart

[162]

Levett, for over 25 years and they have four adult children. Levett and Pia co-authored the book, *Shades of Love: Portraits of Successful Marriages*. Pia was also chosen to join a select group of business experts from around the world, along with business development expert Brian Tracy, to co-write the best-selling book titled, *UNcommon: Common Sense but Uncommon Knowledge from Today's Leading Entrepreneurs and Professionals to Help You Lead an Extraordinary Life of Health, Wealth and Success.*

Pia's passion for giving is evident in her community involvement. She is a volunteer of several community-based organizations and has held numerous leadership roles. She is a member of Alpha Kappa Alpha Sorority, Inc. and the Ventura County chapter of Women's Council of Realtors. As a Certified Referral Trainer (CRT) and member of the Generosity Generation, she is endorsed by North America's Most Referred Real Estate Agent Michael J. Maher, best-selling author of *7 Levels of Communication* and *Miracle Morning for Real Estate Agents* with Hal Elrod. Pia earned a bachelor's degree in finance from The

University of Akron and attended Case Western Reserve University's prestigious Weatherhead School of Management. Pia received her relationship coaching credentials from the Relationship Coaching Institute, is a licensed Realtor with Keller Williams World Class. Consistently a top-ranked speaker at conferences and events, she shares her experiences and knowledge to help others achieve success from the boardroom to the bedroom.

CONTACT PIA
Email: Piawashington@gmail.com

MORE TITLES BY DR. COZETTE M. WHITE:

AVAILABLE ON

AMAZON & Barnes and Noble

- *Attracting the Best: Wealth, Prosperity, and Abundance for Your Life...Now!*
- *Business Formation: The Ultimate Guide to Forming Your LLC*
- *50 Money Mindset Quotes*
- *How the FICO Do I Repair My Credit!?: Guide to Raising Your "Three Digit Number"*
- *Barriers & Bias: Take Control of Your Money: How Woman Can Demand More Money in the Workplace*
- *UNVEILING THE MASK: The Ultimate Guide to Rebound from A Financial Disaster*

CONTACT PUBLISHER:

SBG MEDIA GROUP

https://www.thescatterbrainedgenius.com

www.ingramcontent.com/pod-product-compliance
Lightning Source LLC
Chambersburg PA
CBHW072311210326
41519CB00057B/4092